SOCCER

FROM NEIGHBORHOOD PLAY
TO THE WORLD CUP

★ ★ ★ ★

CAROLINE ARNOLD

Franklin Watts

New York • London • Toronto • Sydney

A First Book • 1991

To Matthew Arnold, who provided inspiration and expert advice for this project and whose enthusiasm for the game has never flagged

Cover photograph copyright © Phil Stephens Photography

Photographs copyright ©: Jon Van Woerden: pp. 6, 37, 48, 58; Cynthia Greer: pp. 14, 18, 22, 27 bottom, 56; Arthur Arnold: pp. 16, 27 top, 39; Action Photography/Bill Cottles: p. 25; Caroline Arnold: p. 32; Sportschrome East/West: p. 33; ASUCLA/Norm Schindler: p. 42; Phil Stephens Photography: pp. 45, 50.

Library of Congress Cataloging-in-Publication Data

Arnold, Caroline.
    Soccer: from neighborhood play to the World Cup / Caroline Arnold.
        p.   cm.   (A First book)
    Includes bibliographical references (p.) and index.
    Summary: Details how to play the game, the various rules, positions of players, and skills required, and presents a brief history of soccer from the days of the Romans to the present-day World Cup championships.
    ISBN 0-531-20037-X
    1. Soccer—Juvenile literature.   (1. Soccer.)   I. Title.
II. Series.
GV943.25.A74   1991
79G.334—dc20   91-12830 CIP AC

CONTENTS

"Soccer is a sport played by young and old, men and women, boys and girls." Although professional teams are for men only, a great number of girls are playing soccer at all levels. In this book, soccer players are often referred to with the use of masculine pronouns; women players, however, are not meant to be excluded.

—C.A.

Argentinean player
Diego Maradona
goes after the ball in a
1990 World Cup game
against Cameroon.

THE SOCCER GAME

On the night of June 8, 1990, the soccer stadium in Milan, Italy, was filled to capacity. The crowd cheered the defending champions, Argentina, led by their captain, Diego Maradona, as they jogged onto the field for the opening game of the World Cup. Everyone expected them to beat the opposing team from Cameroon. In the sixty-year history of the tournament, no black African country had ever won a single game. Yet, when the whistle blew at the end of the game, the team from Cameroon was the winner, by a score of one to zero. It was a dramatic beginning to the fifty-two-game tournament that would ultimately determine the country with the world's best soccer team. For players and fans world-

wide, the World Cup is the most important event in soccer.

The excitement of playing soccer is in trying to control the ball to set up a scoring opportunity; the fun of watching soccer is in seeing how players expertly maneuver the ball to score or to defend their goal. To fully appreciate soccer, it is important to understand how the game is played.

EQUIPMENT

The only essential piece of equipment for soccer is the ball. The usual soccer uniform is a T-shirt, shorts, and socks, and most players wear shoes equipped with cleats, which help to prevent slipping on the field. They also wear shin guards inside their socks to protect against injuries.

In many communities, youngsters begin to play organized soccer as early as kindergarten. Equipment and field sizes are smaller for the younger children and generally are increased in size for older children. By the time players are in their mid-teens, they are playing full-length games on regulation fields.

THE FIELD

The game of soccer is played on a large, rect-angular field, which in Great Britain is often called the "pitch." At each end of the field stands a goal marked by posts 8 yards (7.3 m) apart, a crossbar 8 feet (2.4 m) off the ground, and a net at the back.

The only way to score a point in soccer is by putting the ball into the opposing team's goal. Compared with other sports, soccer is low-scoring, with games often ending in scores of zero to zero or one to zero. Even for highly skilled players, it is not easy to get the ball into a small undefended part of the goal.

Chalk lines drawn around the edge of the soccer field are called the touchlines, or side-lines. A circle in the center of the midfield line marks where the ball is put into play at the beginning of each half and after a goal is scored. At each end of the field are two rec-tangles marking the goal area and the pen-alty area.

Soccer fields vary in size, from 100 to 130 yards (91.4 to 118.9 m) long and 50 to 110 yards (45.7 to 100.6 m) wide. At its maximal size, the

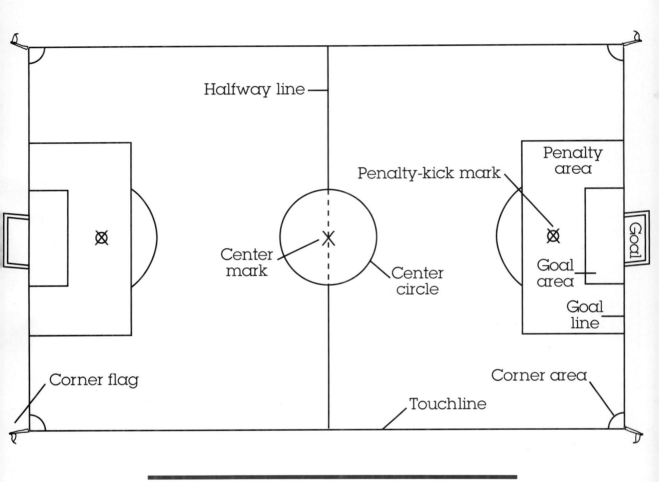

Halfway line —

Penalty area

Penalty-kick mark

Goal

Center mark

Center circle

Goal area

Goal line

Corner flag

Corner area

Touchline

Layout of a soccer field

soccer field is as wide as an American football field is long, and nearly one-third longer. A soccer player needs enormous stamina to run back and forth across such a large space for the duration of a full game.

The regulation time for a soccer game is ninety minutes in two forty-five-minute halves, with a ten-minute break between them. If after this time the game is tied, there may be two short overtime periods. Sometimes a tied game is decided in a "shootout," in which players take kicks from the penalty spot, trying to put the ball past the other team's goalkeeper and into the net.

THE PLAYERS, OFFICIALS, AND COACHES

Each soccer team is made up of eleven players. One player is the goalkeeper, or simply the keeper. He stays in front of the goal and tries to prevent the other team from scoring. The keeper is allowed to touch the ball with his hands as long as he is within the penalty area. Also, he must wear a different-colored shirt from that of the rest of his teammates. This makes it easy to see who is the only player allowed to touch the ball with his hands. He often wears gloves to help catch the ball, and may wear padded shorts to cushion his fall.

The remaining ten players on the soccer team are divided among three positions: defenders, midfielders, and forwards. Each team has its own style of play and arranges its players on the field depending on tactics, the players' abilities, patterns of play, and how their opponent plays.

Most teams line up four defenders, sometimes called fullbacks, across the back of the field in front of their goalkeeper. These defenders are responsible for keeping the ball away from the goal area. Some teams play with one defender, called the sweeper, positioned between the other defenders and the goalkeeper. The sweeper forms the last line of defense, but may also break away from his position and begin a counterattack.

Some teams play with two midfielders and four forwards, others with three or four midfielders and two or three forwards. Usually the ball is passed forward from the defenders to the midfielders, who then pass it to the forwards so that one of them can attempt to score a goal.

Other people on the soccer field are

the officials: the linesmen and the referee. The linesmen watch carefully for penalties, namely, offsides and balls out of play. The referee, however, is the one responsible for enforcing the rules by calling fouls and assessing penalties.

The referee's watch is the official timepiece of the game. Unlike many other sports, once the game begins, play does not stop unless someone is injured. Otherwise, play is continuous, except for short pauses when the ball is kicked out of bounds or when there is a free, or penalty, kick.

The coaches help the team work together to improve skills and to play as a team to score goals and win games.

THE RULES OF THE GAME

The rules of soccer are designed to ensure that the game is played safely and fairly. When a foul is committed or an offsides is called, the referee blows his whistle to signal that play has to stop.

If the ball is kicked completely over one of the sidelines, a member of the team that did not touch it last puts the ball back into play at

**Team captains from Argentina and the
Federal Republic of Germany (West Germany)
meet with officials before the final game
of the 1990 World Cup tournament.**

the point where it went out. He must throw the ball over his head with both hands, and both feet must touch the ground on or behind the sideline.

When the ball goes out over the goal line, and is last touched by an opposing player, the goalkeeper puts it back into play by taking a goal kick rather than throwing it in at the goal line. However, if the defending team puts the ball over its own goal line, the opposing team is given a corner kick (the ball is kicked from the small quarter circle at the corner of the field). Corner kicks provide good opportunities to score; the ball can be sent to the front of the goal and then be kicked or headed in by a teammate.

A free kick is awarded to a player when a member of the opposing team commits a foul (breaks one of the rules). For a major foul, the fouled, or opposing, team is given a direct free kick—the ball may be kicked directly toward the goal without a second player touching it first. The ball is placed where the foul occurred, and all opposing players must stand at least 10 yards (9.1 m) from the ball until it is kicked. Major fouls are considered intentional—kicking, tripping, pushing, hold-

(Left) A young player takes a corner kick.

(Below) Defending players line up in front of the goal in an attempt to block a free kick.

ing, striking, charging, and touching the ball with the hand or arm.

If a major foul is committed within the penalty area, the fouled team is awarded a penalty kick. The ball is placed 12 yards (11 m) from the center of the goal. No other player may stand within the penalty box, and all players must be 10 yards (9.1 m) from the kicker. Until the ball is kicked, the keeper must stand on the goal line and may not move his feet.

Indirect free kicks, which are awarded for minor fouls, cannot go into the goal without the ball first being touched by a second player. Minor fouls include offsides, obstruction, and dangerous plays such as high kicking or trying to play the ball when held by the goalkeeper.

If the referee believes a player has deliberately played in a dangerous manner or is behaving in an unsportsmanlike way, he may caution that player or send him off the field. A caution, or warning, is indicated by a yellow card; a red card means the player must leave the field. A player who receives two yellow cards in the same game is also sent off the field. When a player is sent off, he

The referee gives a cautionary yellow card to an Austrian player during a 1990 World Cup game against the U.S.A.

cannot be replaced. The team must play one person short for the rest of the game.

A player is in an offsides position if he is ahead of the ball in the opponent's half of the field and there are fewer than two opponents between him and the goal at the instant the ball is played forward. The referee calls offsides if, in addition to being in an offsides position, that player is interfering with the play of an opponent or is trying to gain an advantage by being in an offsides position.

Soccer is one of the few games where the referee does not have to call every foul. If the referee believes that by calling the foul he would unfairly penalize the fouled team by taking away its control of the ball, he may choose to let the play continue. This is known as the "advantage" clause because it allows the play to go on despite a foul when a team already has an advantage. Otherwise, a team might commit a foul every time it wanted to stop the game's action.

SOCCER SKILLS

Soccer is a sport that requires every team member to be aware of what is happening on the field, both around and away from the ball. Running, quickness, and clear thinking all play a part in making a good soccer player. Unlike some other sports, in which you must be tall or heavy to be successful, soccer is a sport in which size is not an important factor.

The ability to kick the ball is an obvious soccer skill, but every player must be able to control the ball in various ways. Except for the arms and hands, every part of the body may be used to control the ball and send it on its way.

KICKING

Soccer players kick the ball for long passes, corner and penalty kicks, and goal attempts. When an expert player powers, or maneuvers, the ball into the goal, his whole body works to make it move as fast and as hard as possible. Just as most people are left- or right-handed, a soccer player is left- or right-footed.

For a long kick, the player approaches the ball and places his support foot next to the ball. Then, bending his knees slightly, he kicks the ball with the instep of his other foot. As the ball sails away, the player's leg continues to rise in a follow-through motion.

PASSING

When you watch a professional soccer game, you will notice that no single player keeps the ball for long. Accurate and effective passing is a skill that is developed through practice. A good defender learns to anticipate passes by the other team so that he can deflect or take the ball away. The simplest passes are made with the inside of the foot, but players might

A Federal Republic of Germany player shoots the ball for the winning goal in the 1990 World Cup final game.

also pass with the outside of the foot, depending on where a teammate is located on the field.

DRIBBLING

Sometimes no one is available for a pass and the field is open for a player to run toward the goal with the ball. Running forward while keeping the ball in control is called *dribbling*. The player uses his foot to tap the ball in front of him, fast enough for him to keep running behind it, but not so hard that it gets too far away from him. Midfielders and forwards dribble while getting into position to make a pass or to attempt a shot on the goal. Their bodies twist and turn to shield the ball from other players, to disguise the direction in which they plan to go, and to thread their way through a crowded field. One of the reasons players like Pelé and Maradona are world champions is that they are experts at moving the ball and keeping control of it in what seem like impossible situations. A good practice drill for dribbling is to set up traffic cones, benches, or other obstacles and to try dribbling the ball around them.

HEADING

For people unfamiliar with soccer, it often appears after watching a game that all the players will go home with giant headaches. But this isn't so. When the ball is headed, or hit properly with the forehead, it does not hurt. Players use headers most often near the goal either to score or, if they are defensive players, to clear the ball away from the goal area. Midfield players also use their heads to pass. Just as basketball players looking for rebounds need to leap in the right place at just the right time, successful soccer players depend on good anticipation and accurate timing for heading the ball. It can be scary at first to make your head a target for the ball, and coaches usually wait until children are ready before teaching them this skill.

TRAPPING

A player receiving or intercepting a pass must gain control of the ball before he can do anything with it. *Trapping* is the art of stopping the ball's motion and maneuvering it so that a play can be attempted. On the ground, you

A player leaps high to head the ball in a high-school championship game.

can trap the ball by stopping it with the inside of your foot and pulling back just slightly at the moment of impact to keep the ball from bouncing off your foot. A ball in the air can be trapped with the upper part of your leg or with your chest and upper body. One way to learn ball control is by juggling the ball with the knees and feet. When Pelé was a boy, he did not have a ball so he juggled oranges with his legs, perfecting many of the skills that later made him a star player.

MARKING AND TACKLING

In soccer, guarding an opponent man to man is called *marking*. In marking, each defensive player except the sweeper is responsible for guarding one player on the opposing team and tries to stay between him and the goal. If the opposing player gets the ball, the defender does his best to take it away from him. Other systems of play give each player responsibility for controlling the ball on a certain portion of the field.

Unlike American football, in soccer *tackling* does not mean grabbing another player and forcing him to the ground. Rather, it is the

(Left) Two high-school players vie for control of the ball.

(Below) The Irish goalkeeper dives for the ball in a 1990 World Cup game.

art of taking the ball from another player. One of the most difficult plays in soccer is the slide tackle, in which the ball is kicked out from under a running player. Tackles must be executed properly to avoid being called fouls.

GOALKEEPING

The goalkeeper may kick, catch, or punch the ball to prevent it from going into the net. When a player from the opposing team approaches the goal, the keeper may move forward to narrow the angle from which the player can shoot. The keeper also plays an important role in starting offensive plays from the backfield, either by placing a long kick downfield or by giving the ball to one of the defenders to bring it up the field.

HISTORY OF SOCCER

HOW THE GAME BEGAN

Games in which balls or round objects are kicked, thrown, or punched toward a goal have been played for centuries. Ancient Romans played a game called "harpastum," in which two teams tried to push a ball over lines drawn behind their opponents. Early football games in England were probably played with a ball formed from the bladder of a pig or cow and filled with air; later, the balls were covered with leather. These early games often turned into violent, uncontrolled brawls between large numbers of players.

It was not until the beginning of the nineteenth century that a game resembling soc-

cer began to be played in an organized way. During this time it was introduced as a sport in many English schools. Rules varied from school to school with one exception: the ball could never be touched by a player's hands. In 1823, when a player at a school named Rugby broke this rule by carrying the ball toward the goal, a new game was born— rugby. Football enthusiasts then split into two camps, those who favored rugby and those who preferred to play without the use of their hands. Finally, in October 1863, a group at Cambridge, England, met to decide on a set of uniform rules for the traditional no-hands form of football. This game was called "association football" and became popularly known by its abbreviated name, soccer. In the United States we use the term soccer to distinguish the game from American football, but in many other countries of the world, soccer is still known by the name of football.

In the late nineteenth century, as the British colonized much of the world, they took the game of soccer with them. One of the best features of soccer is that it can be played almost anywhere in almost any kind of weather, can accommodate different numbers of players, and requires no other equipment than a ball. When a ball is not available, players have been known to make a substitute by tying together rags or reeds.

FIFA

Today, soccer is played in almost every country in the world. As soccer became popular, national associations were formed. In 1904, representatives of these associations met in Paris, France, and formed the Fédération Internationale de Football Associations, more commonly known by its initials, FIFA. FIFA is governed by the Executive Committee, composed of twenty-one elected members, with headquarters in Zurich, Switzerland.

In 1930, FIFA organized its first international soccer tournament. The winning team would get the Jules Rimet Cup, the original World Cup trophy, which was given permanently to Brazil in 1970 after it won the tournament for the third time. The present World Cup trophy, first awarded in 1974, now remains in the permanent possession of FIFA. The World Cup competition is held once every four years in even, non-summer Olympic years. All of the 166

**A soccer ball made of dried
banana leaves from Uganda**

The World Cup trophy

member countries in FIFA are eligible to participate in the World Cup preliminary rounds unless they have been disqualified for some reason.

FIFA also supervises the soccer competitions in the Olympic Games. As in the World Cup, qualifying rounds are held in the two years before each Olympics to determine the teams that will play in the Olympic tournament. Unlike the World Cup, in which any professional soccer player is eligible, in the Olympics players must be under twenty-three years of age.

In addition to the World Cup and the Olympics, FIFA sponsors the World Youth Championship for the FIFA/Coca-Cola Cup for players under twenty years of age, the FIFA Under-17 World Tournament, the FIFA Five-a-Side (Indoor) Football World Championship, and the FIFA Women's World Championship.

As in other sports, soccer rules are periodically changed to meet changing circumstances. One change being discussed now is whether to divide the playing time into quarters instead of halves to allow more time for breaks on televised games. Recently, FIFA approved an experimental change in the rules in Chile for the 1991 season. Among other changes, it would abolish offsides and replace throw-ins with kick-ins. If the new rules create more scoring opportunities, they could make soccer a more exciting spectator sport.

YOUTH SOCCER

In November 1989, on a sunny afternoon in Trinidad, Paul Caligiuri, midfielder for the U.S. team, scored the goal that gave the U.S. a spot in the 1990 World Cup tournament. Caligiuri, then twenty-five years old, started playing soccer on an American Youth Soccer Organization (AYSO) team in southern California when he was seven years old. AYSO is one of many organizations in the United States that provide opportunities for youngsters to play soccer and to learn soccer skills. When Paul Caligiuri was young, soccer was just beginning to increase in popularity. Today, soccer is played by more children under the age of twelve than any other sport except basketball.

U.S.A. player Paul Caligiuri

AYSO

AYSO was founded in 1964 in Torrance, California, by five men eager to promote soccer and to provide a positive sports experience for young people. In its first year, AYSO had nine teams in two communities. By 1989, with the celebration of its twenty-fifth anniversary, it had grown to an organization of 500,000 members, with 24,000 teams in thirty-six states plus Washington, D.C., and Puerto Rico. For many children, AYSO is their first soccer experience.

Beginning with Division 7 for children aged five and six years, AYSO has teams for both boys and girls up to the age of eighteen. The teams are co-ed, but there are also independent girls' and boys' teams whenever possible. In 1990, about 96,000 girls participated in AYSO soccer, constituting almost one-third of the registration.

What distinguishes AYSO from most other soccer organizations is its philosophy of "everyone plays." Every child, regardless of ability, plays in at least one-half of every game. The founders of AYSO believe that every child should have the opportunity to

Young AYSO players do the traditional handshake at the end of the game.

learn soccer skills, teamwork, and sportsmanship and to develop confidence and self-esteem by playing, not by being a spectator or sitting on the bench. AYSO tries to keep the competition fair by keeping the teams balanced as to ability so that no team has an unfair advantage.

AYSO also promotes positive coaching, helping kids develop their soccer skills in a constructive way. One of the dilemmas for youth soccer organizations is finding enough coaches. Most adults in the United States did not play soccer when they were young and are unfamiliar with the rules and the skills needed for the game. However, as more parents cheer for their children on the soccer sidelines and learn about soccer in clinics and training sessions, the number of good coaches will grow.

In some communities, recreational soccer programs similar to AYSO are sponsored by parks and recreation departments and by community centers such as the Young Men's Christian Association (YMCA) and Young Women's Christian Association (YWCA). For many people who love soccer, the important part is the opportunity to play, not necessarily to win.

CLUB SOCCER

For children and adults who want to play at a more competitive level, there is club soccer. Both boys' and girls' teams organized by age, as well as men's and women's adult teams, play against each other in competitive leagues. Club teams often travel to tournaments both within and outside the United States. This gives the players the opportunity to develop skills and to play against some of the best soccer players in their age group.

HIGH SCHOOL AND COLLEGE SOCCER

Soccer is the fastest growing sport for high-school students. In Europe and elsewhere outside the United States, talented teenaged soccer players go directly from high school or club teams to professional teams, where they are able to gain the experience needed to become competitive international athletes. In the United States, soccer players, like those in most other sports, get their training in college. Each year, the best college teams play in a tournament sponsored by the National Collegiate Athletic Association (NCAA) to determine the national champion. American col-

**Players battle for the ball in the
1990 NCAA championship game.
UCLA won on penalty kicks by
a score of four to three.**

leges now have more varsity soccer teams than football teams, and the quality of play is becoming stronger. However, since the disbanding of the North American Soccer League in 1985, the best college soccer players have had to go abroad after graduation if they want to pursue professional careers in outdoor soccer.

SOCCER IN THE UNITED STATES

THE U.S. SOCCER FEDERATION

The U.S. Soccer Federation (USSF), headquartered in Colorado Springs, Colorado, is the national organization that oversees soccer in the United States. It supervises and maintains a registration system for thousands of players and referees. It also organizes national cup competitions, manages seven national teams, which compete worldwide, arranges educational courses for coaches and referees, stages international matches, and processes international player transfers.

At national tournaments organized by age, the USSF scouts for players for its national

The U.S.A. women's national team (blue) plays against the U.S.S.R.

teams. The USSF sponsors five men's teams for international competition: the National Team, a Five-a-Side team, and the Under-23, Under-20, and Under-17 teams. For women there are the U.S. Women's Team and the Girls' Under-19 team.

In recent years, many of the U.S. teams have done well. In 1989, the men's Under-20 team placed fourth in the FIFA/Coca-Cola Cup in Saudi Arabia, and the Under-17 team scored an impressive victory over the Brazilian team in Scotland during the World Youth Championship. The U.S. Women's Team won the annual Sardinia Cup in Italy.

The USSF is governed by a twenty-four-member board of directors that represents the three administrative divisions of the organization—youth, amateur, and professional. Once every two years, the members meet to elect a president. In August 1990, they chose Alan Rothenberg, a former owner of the Los Angeles soccer team, the Aztecs, and one of the organizers of soccer at the 1984 Olympics. A presidential term was formerly for two years, but has now been changed to four years beginning with Rothenberg's term.

THE U.S. NATIONAL TEAM

The U.S. National Team represents the United States in the World Cup and other international tournaments. To qualify for the World Cup, the United States team plays teams from an area called the CONCACAF Zone, which includes North and Central America and the Caribbean countries. Two teams represent this zone in the World Cup. In 1989, when the U.S. team went into its last qualifying game against Trinidad and Tobago, the players knew that only a win would earn them a spot at the World Cup. Their previous game against Trinidad and Tobago, which had been played in California, had ended in a tie. Many people thought the U.S. team would lose, but in the most triumphant moment for U.S. soccer in decades, the U.S. team emerged as the victor. It was the first time the U.S. team had qualified for the World Cup in forty years. Only three other times had the U.S. team played in the World Cup tournament—once in 1930, when they placed third, and again in 1934 and 1950.

The 1990 U.S. team, coached by Bob Gan-

The U.S.A. team celebrates after
its victory over Trinidad
and Tobago, November 1989.

sler, was formed almost entirely of college players. These twenty-two men were the second youngest team at the World Cup tournament, and because only a few of them had ever played with professional teams, they were the most inexperienced in international play. Their inexperience showed in their first World Cup game against Czechoslovakia when they were defeated, five to one. However, in their second game against Italy, the U.S. team surprised everyone by almost tying the Italians before losing by a score of one to zero, gaining worldwide respect with this strong showing. Unfortunately, their third and last game, against a strong Austrian team, was a two-to-one loss, which ended the U.S. team's participation in the tournament. With four years to prepare for the next World Cup, the U.S. team expects to improve.

THE OLYMPIC DEVELOPMENT PROGRAM

One reason the United States has not been a strong contender in international soccer is because until recently relatively few U.S. children grew up playing the game. Now, how-

(Top) Members of the U.S.A. team line up before their 1990 World Cup game against Austria. *Left to right, top row:* Tony Meola, Mike Windischmann, Bruce Murray, Marcelo Balboa, Desmond Armstrong, John Doyle. *Bottom row:* Tab Ramos, Peter Vermes, Jimmy Banks, Paul Caligiuri, John Harkes.

(Right) Two players go after the ball during a tournament at an Olympic Development camp in Dallas, Texas.

ever, with more than 12 million children playing soccer, there is a growing pool of talent.

The Olympic Development Program (ODP) is designed to identify the best of these young players and offer them quality training. Candidates ranging in age from fourteen to nineteen (eighteen for boys) go to regional tournaments, where they are evaluated by coaches. The best players are then invited to attend soccer camps, where teams are formed that compete in national tournaments and may travel to Europe to play.

PROFESSIONAL SOCCER IN THE UNITED STATES

The American Soccer League (ASL), the oldest professional league in the United States, was in existence from 1921 to 1984. Another league, the North American Soccer League (NASL), which included such teams as the New York Cosmos and the Los Angeles Aztecs, was the only high-profile outdoor professional soccer league in the United States. After operating for nineteen years, it disbanded in 1985. With it went the hopes of many who had considered it a symbol of the rebirth of soccer as a major sport in the U.S. Since then, two other outdoor leagues have formed, the American Soccer League, with teams in the eastern United States, and the Western Soccer League, with teams in the West. Neither of these leagues, however, offers the same level of play found outside the United States or in the former NASL.

The U.S. Soccer Federation is developing a plan for reorganizing professional outdoor soccer in the United States. Currently, there are three professional indoor leagues. Indoor soccer is played by teams of five players and a goalkeeper in a walled playing area similar to a hockey rink.

THE WORLD CUP

The first World Cup tournament was held in 1930 in Uruguay and has continued every four years since then, except during the war years of 1942 and 1946. Twenty-four national teams play in the month-long tournament. The participating teams include the defending champion, that of the host country, plus twenty-two teams determined by a two-year-long series of qualifying games.

In the December before the tournament, the names of the twenty-four teams are drawn in a lottery to determine the location of the games and who will play whom in the first-round matches. Six groups are formed, composed of four teams each. During the first two weeks, these teams play round-robin matches (in which each team plays every other team) within each group. Teams earn two points for a win, one point for a tie, and no points for a loss.

Sixteen of the twenty-four teams go on to the second round. These include the top two teams from each group, plus the four next-best teams. The teams are selected on the basis of points and, in case of a tie, by various tie-breaking factors. The rest of the tournament is a sixteen-team single-elimination event, with the final match determining the winner of the World Cup.

In 1986, the final game between the Federal Republic of Germany (West Germany) and Argentina was watched on television by nearly 650 million people worldwide—more than five times as many people as watched the American football Superbowl in 1990. More people watch the World Cup soccer tournament in person and on television than any other sporting event.

ITALIA 1990 WORLD CUP

The host for the 1990 World Cup was Italy, a country in which soccer is a national passion.

Games were scheduled in twelve cities, with the opening ceremonies held in Milan and the final match scheduled at the Olympic Stadium in Rome. At the end of the first round, most of the teams that had been predicted to do well had done so. However, the teams from Cameroon and Costa Rica surprised everyone with their successes, while the USSR and Sweden, who had been expected to be strong teams, did not advance. The second-round teams included Italy, Uruguay, Ireland, Romania, Brazil, Argentina, Spain, Yugoslavia, Cameroon, Colombia, England, Belgium, Czechoslovakia, Costa Rica, the Federal Republic of Germany, and The Netherlands.

By the time of the semifinal matches, Italy and Argentina remained in one bracket, and England and the Federal Republic of Germany in the other. All four teams had been previous winners of the World Cup, and all had star-quality players.

During second-round matches, if any game is tied at the end of regulation time, play continues in two fifteen-minute overtime periods. If the game is still tied at the end of overtime, the winner is determined by a penalty kick tiebreaker, or shootout. Players take

**Colorful dancers were part of the
opening ceremonies of the 1990
World Cup tournament.**

turns shooting, one on one, against the goal-keeper. This was the situation at the end of both semifinal matches. Few moments in soccer are more tense, and when the shootouts were over, Argentina had outscored an extremely disappointed Italy, and the Federal Republic of Germany had beaten England. The final match, played on Sunday, July 8, was a repeat match of the 1986 World Cup final, the Federal Republic of Germany versus Argentina. This time, however, the Federal Republic of Germany outplayed Argentina and won, 1-0, by a goal scored on a penalty kick resulting from a controversial play.

WORLD CUP U.S., 1994

In 1994, for the first time in history, the World Cup tournament will be played in the United States, and as the host country of the event, the U.S. team will automatically have a place in the tournament. Despite the fact that soccer is not a traditional spectator sport in the United States, it is expected to be a popular event. In 1984, when the Olympics were held in the United States, 1.4 million fans attended the soccer games, and more than 100,000 came to

(Right) In a dramatic shootout, English goalkeeper Peter Shilton was unable to prevent his team's 1990 World Cup semifinal loss to the Federal Republic of Germany.

(Below) Members of the victorious 1990 World Cup championship team from the Federal Republic of Germany display their medals and the winners' trophy.

the final matches at the Rose Bowl in Pasadena, California, setting records for attendance at a soccer game in this country.

The 1994 World Cup games will be played at a maximum of twelve and a minimum of eight stadiums throughout the country. Most stadium fields, which are designed for football, will have to be enlarged to meet soccer specifications. Making the World Cup tournament a financial and popular success will be a challenge in the United States, a country where people are not accustomed to watching professional soccer. The president of the 1994 Organizing Committee for the World Cup is Scott LeTellier, whose experience includes being involved with the 1984 Olympic soccer games. One of the vice-chairmen of the committee is former secretary of state Henry Kissinger, a longtime soccer fan.

Soccer is a universal sport played and loved by more people in the world than any other game. Soccer enthusiasts hope that the excitement generated by the 1994 World Cup games in the United States will propel U.S. soccer to a truly professional level, equal to that of the rest of the world.

THE WORLD CUP

		Final Match	
Year	**Host Country**	**Winner/Loser**	**Score**
1930	Uruguay	Uruguay/Argentina	4-2
1934	Italy	Italy/Czechoslovakia	2-1
1938	France	Italy/Hungary	4-2
1950	Brazil	Uruguay/Brazil	2-1
1954	Switzerland	Federal Republic of Germany/Hungary	3-2
1958	Sweden	Brazil/Sweden	5-2
1962	Chile	Brazil/Czechoslovakia	3-1
1966	England	England/Federal Republic of Germany	4-2
1970	Mexico	Brazil/Italy	4-1
1974	Federal Republic of Germany	Federal Republic of Germany/The Netherlands	3-1
1978	Argentina	Argentina/The Netherlands	3-1
1982	Spain	Italy/Federal Republic of Germany	3-1
1986	Mexico	Argentina/Federal Republic of Germany	3-2
1990	Italy	Federal Republic of Germany/Argentina	1-0
1994	U.S.		

FOR FURTHER READING

Gutman, Bill. *Soccer: Start Right and Play Well.* Lakeville, CT: Grey Castle, 1989.

——. *Modern Soccer Superstars.* New York: Putnam, 1980.

Laitin, Ken and Steve. *The World's Number One Selling Soccer Book.* New York: Messner, 1981.

Riley, John. *Soccer.* Englewood Cliffs, N.J.: Silver Burdett, 1987.

Sullivan, George. *Better Soccer for Boys and Girls.* New York: Putnam, 1983.

Widdows, Richard. *The Soccer Book.* New York: Octopus, 1981.

INDEX